HOLIDAYS: THEN AND NOW

Written by Lucy M George
Illustrated by Alexander Wilson

Contents

Beside the …
A one-day holiday 4
The tourist trade 6
Early beach fashion 8
The age of the car 10
Seaside fun 12
Flying overseas 14
A Spanish summer holiday 16
Up, up and away! 18
Into the future 20
Glossary 21
How holidays have changed 22

Collins

Beside the seaside

What do you think of when you imagine a seaside holiday?

bucket and spade

sand

Let's look at how summer holidays began, and what they are like today.

sea

ice cream

A one-day holiday

In the 1900s, train travel in the UK became cheaper.

More people could afford to take a day trip to the seaside.

Off to the coast

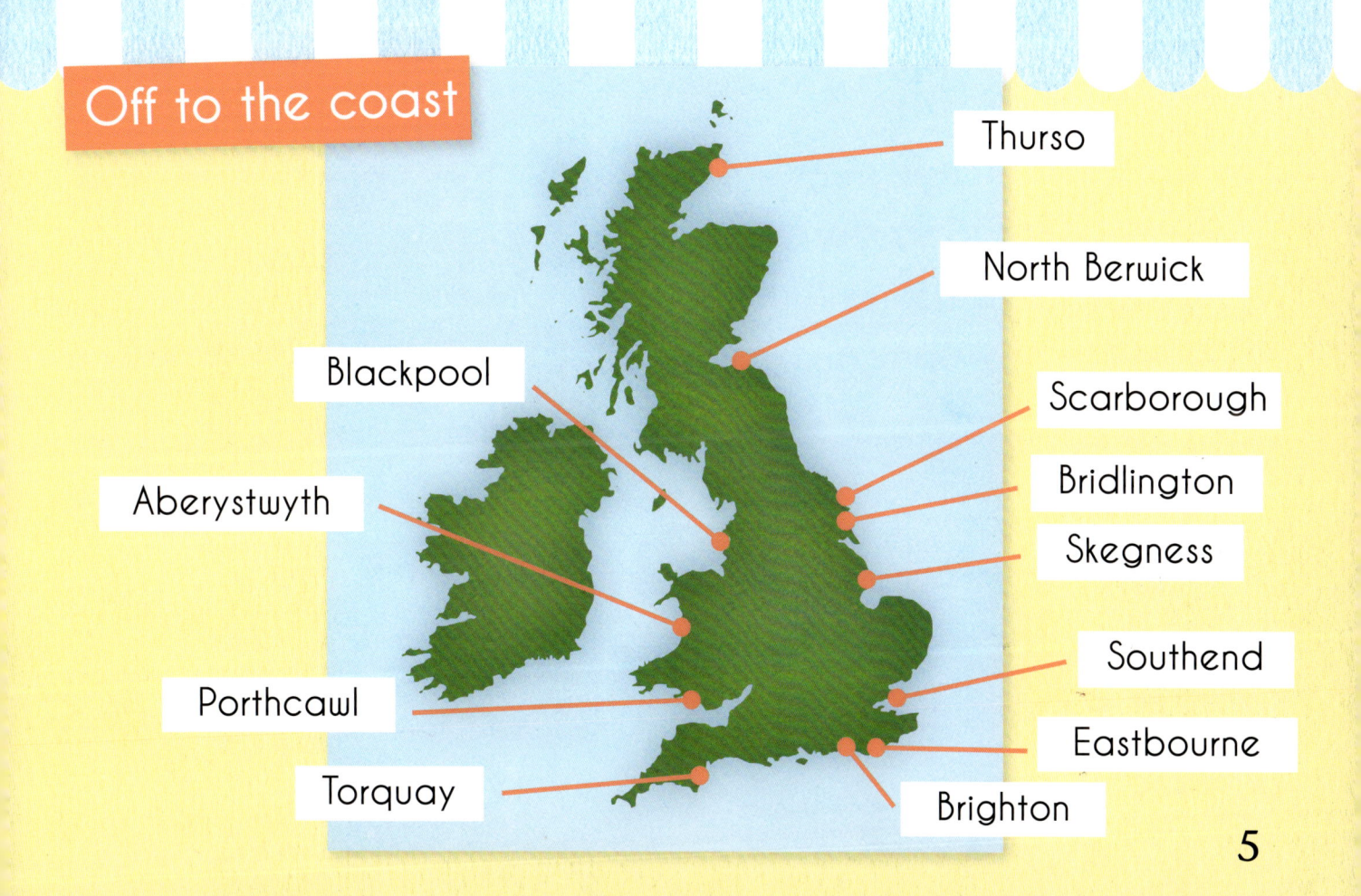

- Thurso
- North Berwick
- Scarborough
- Bridlington
- Skegness
- Southend
- Eastbourne
- Brighton
- Torquay
- Porthcawl
- Aberystwyth
- Blackpool

5

The tourist trade

Seaside towns made money from **tourists**. They started to give these **holidaymakers** more things to spend their money on.

beach huts to change clothes in

shows on the pier

deck chairs

7

Early beach fashion

1900s

Bathing suits covered the chest and legs.

1910s

1920s

These clothes made it easier for women to swim.

Swimsuits were sleeveless, but still covered the tops of the legs.

9

The age of the car

From the 1950s, more people had cars. They could go anywhere they liked. Holidays might even have lasted up to a week.

Holidaymakers could stay in a …

caravan

tent

holiday camp

11

Seaside fun

Some seaside tourists stayed in a hotel or a **guest house**.

Donkey rides and Punch and Judy shows took place on the beach.

Time for lunch!

- lemonade
- sandwiches
- hard-boiled eggs
- cake

13

Flying overseas

In the 1970s, cheaper air travel meant people started to take summer holidays abroad.

Spain was the most popular place to go on holiday.

Welcome to Spain

15

A Spanish summer holiday

The weather in Spain is much hotter than in the UK.

The hotels are huge!

This is a **flamenco** dancing show.

There are new water sports to try.

17

Up, up and away!

By the 1980s, it had become possible to fly almost anywhere in the world.

Bigger planes could carry more passengers. Aircraft could travel for longer distances. Tickets were cheaper.

19

Into the future

Today, there are lots of different holidays to choose from.

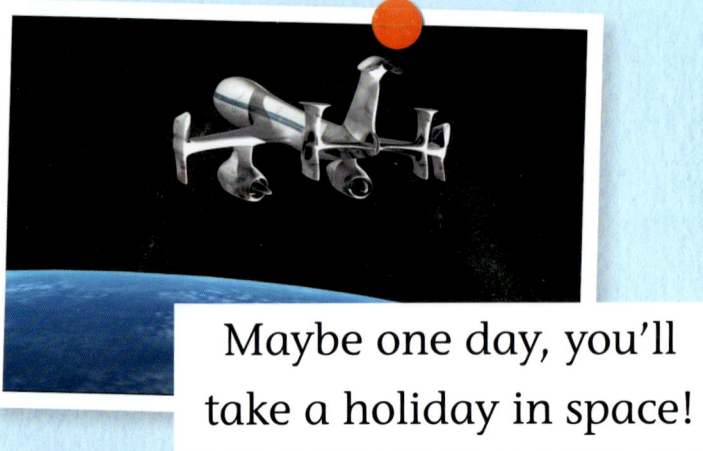

Some people go on activity holidays.

Some people explore jungles or deserts.

Maybe one day, you'll take a holiday in space!

Glossary

flamenco
a traditional Spanish dance

guest house
a house where tourists can stay

holidaymakers
people on holiday away from home

tourists
people who visit somewhere for a holiday

How holidays have changed

1920s | 1950s

around the UK by train

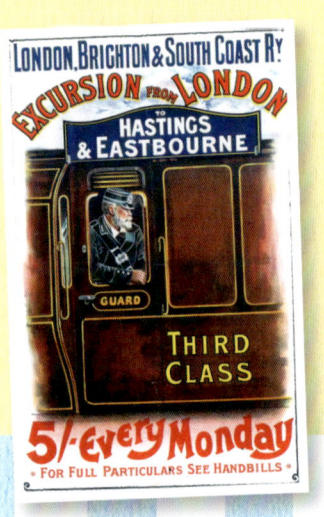

around the UK by car

22

| 1970s | 1980s | 21st century |

around Europe by aeroplane

around the world by aeroplane

into outer space?

Ideas for reading

Written by Clare Dowdall, PhD
Lecturer and Primary Literacy Consultant

Reading objectives:
- predict what might happen on the basis of what has been read so far
- apply phonic knowledge and skills as the route to decode words
- make inferences on the basis of what is being said and done

Spoken language objectives:
- use spoken language to develop understanding through speculating, imagining and exploring ideas
- give well-structured descriptions, explanations and narratives for different purposes
- use relevant strategies to build their vocabulary
- articulate and justify answers, arguments and opinions

Curriculum links: History; Geography

Interest words: caravan, fashion, flamenco, guest house, holidaymakers, passengers, popular, tourists

Word count: 230

Resources: audio-recorder for radio advert, pencils and paper

Build a context for reading

This book can be read over two or more reading sessions.

- Look at the front cover and read the title aloud. Ask children to predict what this information book will be about, using the clues in the illustrations.
- Turn to the back cover and read the blurb aloud. Ask children to describe what their holidays are like and how holidays might have been different in the past (refer to older friends and relatives).

Understand and apply reading strategies

- Turn to pp2–3. Ask a volunteer to read the text. Revise how to tackle longer words that contain more than one syllable. Remind children to break words into known and unknown chunks and to use phonic strategies (i-mag-ine/hol-i-day).